S45857

LONDON BOROUGH OF ENFIELD
LIBRARY SERVICES

This book to be RETURNED on or before the latest date stamped
...ss a renewal has been obtained by personal call, post or
...one, quoting the above number and the date due for return.

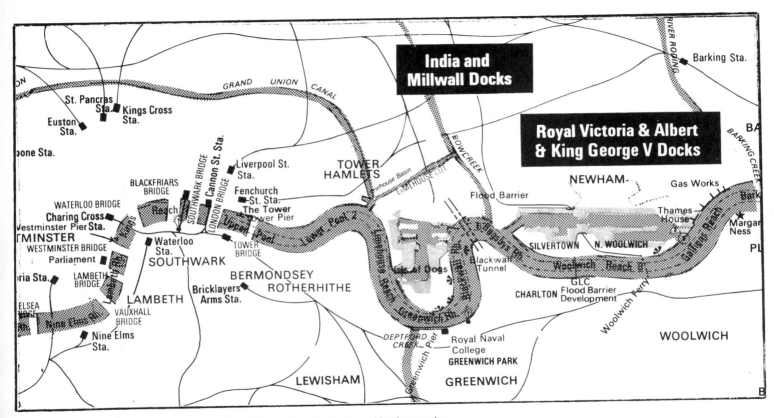

Contemporary map of the section of the Thames described in Harry Harris memoirs

UNDER OARS

Reminiscences
of a Thames Lighterman
1894-1909

Harry Harris

I wish to dedicate this book to all those people who
believe that water transport has a vital part to play
in an integrated transport system.

Published by Centerprise Trust Ltd.
c/o 136-138 Kingsland High Street, London E.8
and Stepney Books Publications
c/o 196 Cable Street, London E1
Text and foreword © Bob Harris 1978
Illustrations © Albert Rolles 1978
Production: Denise Jones and Ken Worpole
ISBN   0 903738 35 X
Printed by Interlink Longraph Limited, 45 Mitchell Street, London EC1.

FOREWORD

My father was born in 1880 at 77, Park Street, Southwark. Leaving school at 13 he was apprenticed to his father Charles Harris, a Freeman of the Watermen and Lightermen's Company to 'learn his Art, and with him (after the manner of an Apprentice) to dwell and serve upon the River Thames from the Day of the Date hereof, until the full End and Term of Seven years...'.

During this period of apprenticeship he had pledged nor to marry 'nor play at Cards, Dice, Tables,' nor or 'haunt Taverns or Play Houses, nor absent himself from his Master's Service Day nor or Night.' In return his father and master 'shall teach and instruct or cause to be taught and instructed, finding unto the said Apprentice Meat, Drink, Apparel, Lodging, and all other Necessaries according to the Custom of the City of London.' Witnessed by two members of the Court at Watermen's Hall Mr. W. S. Page and Mr. A. Sales and by the Clerk Mr. L. S. White, these indentures allowed young Harry Harris to start his career on the River as an apprenticed Waterman and Lighterman on the fourteenth of August 1894. Seven years later he became the sixth generation of his family to be a Freeman of the Company of Watermen and Lightermen of the River Thames as forty-one years later I became the seventh.

Father worked for small or family-owned Lighterage firms. There were few tugs about; most of the transportation of goods up and down the River was done in lighters — dumb barges with a fixed rudder or 'budget' — able to carry from fifteen to one hundred and twenty tons of cargo, propelled by wind and tide and manned by Lightermen, capable of rowing with oars up to thirty feet in length. This art of navigation, known as 'driving under oars', is possibly unique in Great Britain and requires great skill and knowledge of local conditions and tidal sets.

A punt, no near relation to its Cam or Cherwell namesake, with a registered tonnage of up to twenty-nine and three-quarter tons, was able to carry fifty tons of cargo and could be 'driven under oars' by one man. Built of wood, with flared sides to make them handy, these craft were slightly beamier forward than aft, hence the saying on the River 'where her head will go so will her stern'. These punts were the work-horses of the Edwardian Thames in the days of close-knit riverside communities at Wapping, Shadwell, Ratcliffe Cross, Limehouse and Blackwall on the North side, and Greenwich, Deptford, Horsley Down, Battlebridge, and Bankside on the South.

This book, written by a lighterman about his work and pleasures on and around the River between 1894 and 1909, would not be complete without the illustrations so beautifully drawn by Mr. Albert Rolles, himself a retired lighterman. To Albert many thanks.

In 1935, at the age of 55, my father then a foreman lighterman for Humphrey & Grey Ltd. at Tilbury Dock and responsible for his firm's work there, penned these memoirs, not expecting that they would ever be published or that they would be the subject of an exhibition at the Bear Gardens Museum, Bankside, Southwark in 1974. He was a man of simple tastes loving his family and life as he loved his River Thames. If alive today he would be indignant and angry at the lack of use of this free source of transportation energy, this ever moving, multi-lane, East to West highway, the **River Thames.**

Bob Harris

ACKNOWLEDGEMENTS

For help and interest in this book I would like to thank Bob and Frances Drewer, Jack Faram, Peter Ferguson, Jean Pigrum, Albert Rolles, Brian Sanderson, Celia Stubbs, Jack Tellis, Tom Willets, and the Company of Watermen and Lightermen of the River Thames. Thanks also to all the Harris family for their patience, help, and encouragement.

INTRODUCTION

In the manuscript which forms the substance of this book, 'Under Oars', Harry Harris wrote of his childhood in Southwark, and of his years as a lighterman on the Thames at the turn of the century. The manuscript — pages of copper-plate handwriting in a large ledger book — was given to us by his son, Bob Harris, a lighterman himself today, after one of us had talked about the local publishing work of Centerprise and Stepney Books Publications.

There are several reasons why we are particularly pleased to have published this set of reminiscences. The first arises from the aims which both local publishing groups hold in common, which are to encourage the recording, writing and publishing of working people's experiences which otherwise would remain unrecorded and hence lost to subsequent generations. 'Under Oars' is a valuable addition to the much wider history now being created, particularly that concerning the experience of work and the social and cultural life of working class communities.

We also hope that this account will find a responsive and understanding readership amongst those whose lives have been connected with the work of the London riverside communities, and who will no doubt have had experiences to add to those of Harry Harris in order to fill out a broader picture. For together with Bob Harris and other lightermen, we hope in the next two years to work on producing a much larger book documenting the history of the lighterage industry on the Thames, coming right up to date and even adding some proposals for the future of the industry. We would very much welcome any contributions from Lightermen, Watermen, Tugmen and their families towards providing a comprehensive account of this unique industry, especially in this century. Those people who would like to write something, or who would be prepared to talk to us about their experiences, are warmly invited to get in touch with either of the two publishing projects.

In addition, we would like to draw the attention of those interested in the future of the river and canal industries to the activities and policies of the Transport on Water organisation (TOW), set up and financed themselves by people working in the lighterage industry to encourage the return of freight to the river and the greater use of the river's enormous resources. Given the current concern with diminishing natural resources for transportation, the arguments of the TOW committee should be regarded with some importance.

Finally, we would like to put on record our own appreciation of Harry Harris's memoirs, written now some forty years ago. It is a remarkable document in its own right and brings alive the real person, part of whose life it recorded. It convincingly, and without any over-stressed sense of self-importance, describes in detail the acquisition of a skill, characteristic of many working class trades in practice during the period he wrote about. In recent decades many large scale industrial processes have almost rendered the idea of 'skilled' work obsolete, and we have yet to count the human costs which these processes have meant. What comes across so clearly in 'Under Oars' is the strongly felt sense of personal skill and responsibility exercised on the river, which is also felt as a genuine sense of individual freedom. Ironically, often characterising each other as 'hands', the lightermen in fact use every faculty they possess to go about their work safely, efficiently, and, frequently, enjoyably.

The long section describing in detail one particular journey by lighter under oars from Nine Elms to the Royal Albert Dock is quite extraordinary and shows the complexity and variety of skills and experiences which such a journey demanded. It also reveals a delight in work, reminding us perhaps of one of the widely used precepts which adorned the trade union banners of that time: 'Hope in work, joy in leisure'. That aspiration to find meaning and hope in one's working life urgently needs reclaiming today.

We stand today at a crucial point in our general industrial life, and the dilemma of the lighterage industry, and the people who work in it, is symptomatic of a much larger social dilemma. It seems we can either choose to allow powerful economic forces to completely determine what happens to our cities, work-places, and the places where we live, or we have to decide to re-order the priorities which so radically affect the quality and meaning of our lives. Put simply, it may be a case of either sitting back and in some years' time finding ourselves in a congested and inhuman capital city divided by a completely unused major river, or we have to work towards reversing current trends and insist on putting more freight and work back on to the river, giving our streets and roads more breathing space for people. It is a great contribution that Harry Harris made in his collection of reminiscences to have described so vividly a period when the London riverside communities were alive and thriving, and what has been in the past can help us realise what might be possible, if we so wish it, in the future.

Centerprise
Stepney Books Publications

1 CHILDHOOD AT BANKSIDE, SOUTHWARK 1880—1894

I was born on August 2nd 1880, the eldest son of Charles and Elizabeth Harris, (nee Potkin). Father was the third child of Alfred Thomas Harris who fathered twelve children. My paternal grandparents were alive when I was a child and I was ever keen to hear grandfather's yarns about his years of experiences on the River. Mother's parents were both dead. Her father had died leaving young children, and friends had bought the widow a mangle, a heavy contraption of a box loaded with paving stones for ballast which worked to and fro on large wooden rollers, 'Armstrong' being the motive power. Mother told us that when really up against the fact of having no money for the day's food, they would decide to do somebody's clothes then take these to the house in the hope of being paid. If a mangling bill came to fourpence-halfpenny they were a good — if not the best — customer.

We children were seven: Florence Elizabeth, Harry Thomas, Alice Emily, Eva Louise, Charles Edward, Alfred John and Margaret Ellen (twins). Our home was 77 Park Street, Southwark, all the family being born there. My earliest recollection is that of being taken to St. Saviour's Church, now 'Southwark Cathedral', between the ages of two and three. Then I remember going to school at about the same age; I believe that we all went to school at about two and a half years of age, at least in our family.

I was fairly intelligent and in the course of my school days skipped a 'Standard', as the forms or classes were then called, and was always in a 'Standard' with boys a year older than I. The school was St. Peter's National School. The fee was threepence a week, payable Mondays. The London School Board with free education was by then in existence but our school was thought to be nicer; we used to feel a step higher in the social scale than a 'board school boy'. A conjuror used to obtain permission to hold a 'Seance' after school hours and when this was due the speculation amongst the boys was, 'Shall I be allowed a penny to see the performance?'

There was no playground other than streets, our nearest green being St. James Park. Our Sunday School treats were eagerly anticipated, a whole day on the grass in the country, or what was green fields then. Our chief attraction was Bankside. This was out of bounds to me and almost all children, owing to the unrestricted opportunities of getting 'overboard'. I soon learnt every inch of the Bank and knew where to hide when the tide was out and where to climb ashore other than the landing stairs if Father was seen or reported. He had a way of inspecting one's shoes and could always tell by the mud or chalk adhering to them if I had been 'up the

Bank'. One's shoes got perhaps more blacking on this account. With friends, chiefly sons of Watermen and Lightermen, we soon made free of boats that were not actually in use, so naturally we became boat-minded at an early age.

I managed to swim when ten years old, and, having the river and boats at our disposal, we would have wonderful times in and on the river after school hours in the summer. The best bathe was at low water, the river then being clear and fresh. We would undress on the shore and wallow in the clear river until the Thames Police were sighted, then scramble ashore trying to get a dry shirt over a wet body. I am sure now that being at home in the water is essential to any person working on craft or any waterside occupation. Several times I have been overboard, all except one, accidents. There are three occasions when swimming and keeping my head have saved my own life.

In 1887 the Jubilee of Queen Victoria was celebrated. Our family, as true Watermen, celebrated this by Father taking us and other members of the family to Richmond and back in a rowing boat. I can distinctly remember Putney as it then seemed, clean houses and waving trees, and thinking that one must be rich to live there.

The chief events on the river in my schooldays, other than the Varsity race and the Doggett's Coat and Badge, included the Shah of Persia's visit to London on a steam yacht escorted to Westminster by Torpedo boats, whose Commanders got in rather a pickle in their navigation of this part of the river. I can also remember a Captain Paul Boyton who was putting on a show at Earls Court with Canadian Lumbermen. He arranged for these men to embark at Chelsea, some on logs or a series of logs, jumping from log to log on a rolling movement. There were also Canadian Indians in frail bark canoes dressed in war paint and feathers. These people came down on the tide to London Bridge and some of the log rollers came to grief but were rescued.

Bankside Regatta was an annual event and caused great local excitement, and partisan feeling ran higher than even at election time. I remember that once when a favourite was rowing third and passing close inshore against the tide off Barclay Perkins Wharf, empty beer barrels were flung at the leading sculler as a gentle hint to ease up. A brass band used to follow or attempt to follow the races, the band being seated on the top of a disused tram placed in a barge's hold and towed behind a small tug. This towed barge could not keep up with the race and when about half the course was completed she turned round and met the race as they, the rowers, returned, always arranging to be in at the finale to play 'See the conquering hero comes'. The Collector-in-Chief for the Regatta was also the organiser, a Lighterman called Bobby Bush. On Regatta days after a heat had been decided he would come ashore with the band and march along Bankside and down Emerson Street. He would march ahead, dressed in breeches, silk stockings and buckle shoes, looking straight ahead, keeping time with the band, dignity and importance personified.

Bankside Regatta was an annual event

A comic paper called 'Ally Sloper' (Ally Sloper's Half Holiday) was then a popular weekly issue. Bush would arrange with the publishers to send a person dressed as 'Ally Sloper', being the facsimile of this character. He would have a bottle labelled 'Unsweetened' protruding from the coat pocket, an umbrella of the gamp variety, and a vermilion coloured nose. He would do some clowning along Bankside being followed by hundreds of kiddies, then on to the Grand Stand of disused trams to blow kisses to the girls and encourage the rowers by offering the 'Unsweetened'.

Sometime about 1888 or 1889 Grandfather and Grandmother were elected as Almshouse Pensioners and went to live in the Dulwich Almshouses. He used to visit us often. We were also taken down there occasionally. Grandfather was always speaking of his river days, of his brothers and father and forebears. I very much regret that only a few of his recollections were retained by me. He spoke of such things as being chosen for an oarsman in the Skinners' Company's state barge and of the Bargemaster assuring him that 'as long as I am Master here, you, young Harris shall row an oar in this barge'. His brothers were finely built men and as Watermen knew their regular 'fares' well. A sculptor (famous apparently) being impressed with the finely proportioned figure of his brother Jack Harris, arranged for him to sit as a model for a perfect torso. As a lad he had gone with older brothers to bring a new barge from a yard in Battersea to Bankside. He was not of an age to be allowed to go in with them to the pub to celebrate the launch, so being tired of the long wait occasioned by the celebration, and aware of the danger of grounding as the tide was ebbing, he got under way and brought the brand new barge down the river alone. When one realises that old Battersea Bridge with its narrow wooden arches was then standing, and of course Vauxhall Bridge with nine arches and three distinct sets of tide on the ebb, one can fully appreciate the initiative and skill required, but as he 'breathed boats' when born it can be understood. When he arrived with the new barge his brothers were waiting and ready to explode, but after a close scrutiny of every inch of new paint said, 'Don't you ever do that again.'

He used to boast of being the first foot passenger over Blackfriars Bridge which was then a toll bridge. A contempt for steam tugs was always shown by remarks such as 'Bah, a wooden post would make a Lighterman nowadays.' He resented the fact that any person other than a licensed man could own and trade barges on the river; his name for these owners was 'woodmongers'. Their registration number at Waterman's Hall was always four figures or over — the licenced owners' numbers being three figures or under. The term 'woodmonger' is now extinct, as practically all river trade is carried by companies, some still possessing the three figure number or less.

Grandfather was for a long time Foreman for the widow of a Mr. Chantler, his previous employer; their registration number by the way was No. 1. This business was managed by him virtually, and many clients thought he was the owner, but with pride he would relate his faithful service, accounting for every penny received and spent.

He was born in 1823 before the advent of the railway in London. On one occasion he walked to Brentford from Southwark to bring a barge down river. Upon his arrival it was discovered that he had forgotten the toll money which should have been collected by boat at Kew on the journey down. He then walked back to Southwark, obtained the tolls, strolled back again to Brentford to come away the following tide to row the barge down to London.

Speaking of Old London Bridge, he would tell me of nervous passengers (fares) who would be landed at the upper side of the bridge, re-joining the boat again on the lower side to avoid the danger of shooting the bridge on a strong spring tide. However, as London Bridge was commenced in 1825 and finished in 1831, this was probably told to him, although the old bridge was not demolished until the new bridge was finished.

In his young days, fishermen used to obtain fish from the river. These men were not licensed. 'As awkward as a fisherman' was a term applied in a derogatory sense to any person who was naturally awkward. My mother had several phrases to meet all occasions, those I remember were three:
'You're as artful as Kate Mullet'
'Not if you are as big as Goliath'
'I'll see your neck as long as my arm first', then after a pause, 'and then you shan't'.

I remember the horror we children had of certain Sunday mornings when it had been decided that 'opening' medicine was overdue. For instance, the Saturday before Christmas was a certain date, another was a day before the annual holiday. Mother would mix Jalep with water in a jug then pour out a dose into the Jalep cup — one kept for this purpose. To get the full benefit it was kept stirred as the residue settled quickly. It was awful to take, and to enforce swallowing, the nose was firmly grasped by mother's strong fingers until one gulped the black-brown mess. If one of the children dallied a bit he or she was compelled to drink the residue with the addition of more water and another stir. As this medicine had to be taken first thing, and as I was growing into an artful age, one morning I sensed that this was **it** — the day for the Jalep. I got up early and was a good boy for Mother, busying about the fireplace, getting the knives and forks out and so managing to have breakfast with Mother, thus dodging the issue — but I only caught her out once. The effect of the medicine was to make us ill until the afternoon; the worse one became was held to be sure proof of how much the purge was needed. We are none the worse, so perhaps it really was beneficial. Our parents thought so, and at that time of obedience to their views we hoped so.

The twins were born in Derby Day, 1890, 'Sanfoin's' year. Father had been to the races with an organised outing by a four horse coach or brake. He was apprised of the event somewhere near home and alighted near

Park Street. I met him at the street door saying excitedly, 'Father, Mother's got a baby and there's two.' I learned years after that he was told by dumb show from friends who were looking out for the coach, by rocking an imaginary babe then poking two fingers in the air. When the twins were eight weeks old we all went to Yarmouth by boat for the annual holiday. The babies were in a bassinet, this being stowed in the shelter deck near the sponson[1]; an Italian with his wife and piano organ were also in this vicinity. We kiddies had a great time trying to grind tunes from this instrument. This trip to Yarmouth was for several years an annual holiday and must have required a lot of saving and careful spending for our parents. Sometimes Father would manage a week with us, but if I remember correctly, this was an exception. When one realises that his wages were then about £2.10.0 per week it was wonderful. Father never smoked and was an abstainer from drink, his chief reason I understood being the unselfish regard of his own needs and both parents doing their utmost for the children. Before the birth of the twins, two boy cousins who had lost their mother came to live with us; also, three of Father's sisters, who on account of their parents going to live at Dulwich were without a home. The most appropriate comment on this is 'Mother was a brick'.

I joined the choir at St. Peter's about this period (late 1880's) remaining until leaving school. We were all good boys in that choir, the only indiscretion at service was to roll a marble from top boy to bottom boy along the book rest. This was an art and could only be done when the organ was loud: the 'Te Deum' was a signal. Two friends named Openshaw were in that choir, their father being manager of a seed-crushing mill (Sadlers) in Great Guilford Street. We would be smuggled into the premises and suspect that we became unpopular with the work people. A large tank for some reason, either exhaust or feed, was on top of the building. The water, always being hotter than a hot bath, we would bathe in this. It was parted off by cross bars making a series of squares: diving in one square and trying to miss two and come up in the fourth square was the usual practice. The effect was faces similar to boiled lobster. Then perhaps straight to church for Wednesday evening service, the bathers' rosy faces standing conspicuously enough by contrast to the white surplice for the Vicar to smile and remark how well those boys looked.

---

[1]The triangular platform before and abaft a paddle wheel.

2 WATERMAN AND LIGHTERMAN
The 2 years of Unlicenced Apprenticeship 1894—1896

At the age of thirteen, having passed the seventh, or top Standard, I was asked, 'What do you want to be?' The answer was obvious. Aunt Louie wondered whether Harry boy would like to become a missionary? I said a lighterman, or perhaps go to sea? I was then warned about the discomfort and dangers of these last two jobs. The true story was related about a ship-wrecked crew eating the boy. Rather cheekily, she was reminded that missionaries had met the same fate.

Father was then Foreman for W. Pells & Son and had an opportunity of having me with him to get some experience, or perhaps a warning, before the actual apprenticeship. In June 1894 I saw the opening of the Tower Bridge by the Prince of Wales, later Edward VII, who was aboard the leading vessel. A large number of guests were invited by the firm to view the scene from one of Pells' barges moored on the roads[1] below London Bridge, and refreshments were provided. I was the boat boy and was busy with the passengers to and fro. Pocket money was scarce in those days for me, but I was not allowed to accept any reward or tips. I can still feel the itch in my hand to pick up the sixpences and coppers from the thwart,[2] as well as the sinking feeling of the tummy as Father frowned and gave a negative nod.

On the 14th August 1894 I was apprenticed to Father. He was delighted with his reception at Watermen's Hall. Several members of the court cordially shook hands with him, he murmuring in a low aside their names and qualifications to me. An opening was found for employment, a brother Foreman friend wanted a handy boy, so arrangements were made for me to commence at 12/- per week. After two weeks' work, the Governor, having seen me, decided that my size boy was only worth 10/- and this was offered. Father was indignant, so he took me into his firm for 12/- per week. I honestly believe that he feared spoiling me, hence the training, at least, was spartan.

The following winter, 1894-95 was the coldest for years, the river becoming unnavigable owing to the ice. Heavy snow had fallen in the London district. The local vestries (before the L.C.C. was formed), including the City Council, dumped the snow into the river. Every bridge and embankment saw this dumping going on day after day. This quickly froze together forming ice floes, true ice from the fresh water upper reaches coming down river again to freeze to the floating snow. In my opinion this dumping was a contributory cause to the conditions prevailing on the river that winter. The ice adhered to barges' bottoms, craft grounding 'all

---

[1] buoyed moorings for lighters
[2] seat

shapes'. Many broke adrift and were to be seen floating up or down river. It was peculiar to stand on a bridge to watch what should have been a barge 'athwart the buttress'. However, before reaching the bridge the ice between would act as a fend-off; there would be some loud crunching of ice and then through the bridge-hole she went.

I have seen a fish-cutter, bound for Billingsgate, blow its whistle for Tower Bridge to open, then, as high water came, the bridge opened but the vessel found itself unable to move, although going full ahead: it was just stuck solid in the ice. The bridge then closed until the tide came away, when the ice would liven with the tide and the ship then coming ahead and through. We used to fiddle about, waiting for certain opportunities of clear water to get craft about. On one occasion one of our men refused to stay with a barge at Shadwell, his excuse was a 'defective stove'. So off I had to go. But, I found a good friend in an old lighterman (Harry Mitchell) who had a cosy cabin near, so everybody was satisfied. Even if the whole cargo had been stolen, I should have been none the wiser, having turned in about 7 p.m. until daylight.

It was peculiar how the ice disappeared when the thaw came with the rain. The floes could not have melted so quickly; they must have sunk. The lightermen however, cared little how it had quickly vanished, all being anxious to see the end of this period.

The following summer a vacancy occurred for a lad in the firm of H. Grey Jn. I went there to work principally to gain an insight into the Quay Lighterage trade. This term implies that the master lighterman is bonded by an amount to H. M. Customs to conform to all customs regulations. He is allowed by them to carry dutiable cargoes, removals under bond, and transhipments.

I remember, as one does, my first attempt at the day's work. Being sent to Fresh Wharf to assist an old lighterman with a barge down to London Dock, Shadwell, I said, 'Good morning, Mr. Corps.' He gave me one glance saying, or rather growling, 'What do you want?' I answered in the river parlance, 'I'm your mate.' Contempt for my far from robust figure brought the question, 'Does your schoolmaster know that you are not at school today?' 'Yes, thank you,' I replied. The soft answer did not turn away wrath; he told me not to be saucy to elders.

We started our journey down, I anxious to make a good impression after a somewhat discouraging start. 'Take your oar aft,' was the first order. This operation looks simple but can only be performed by the initiated. The handle is grasped in one hand, the other hand canting[1] the blade with a turn of the wrist causing the blade to plane away from the barge's side. If this canting was not done the oar would come parallel to the gunwale,[2] the handle would go beyond one's reach and either the oar had to be released or into 'the ditch' you would go with the oar. Now I was taught this when a schoolboy taking rides with Father and as I had already

---

[1]slanting   [2]Barge's deck

had two years strenuous training with him I could handle and balance an oar with the next. Running along the narrow gunwale with the oar 'as far as the quarter' I chose the point of balance and with a quick weigh down of the handle threw the oar into its working position against the stern post in less time than these words were penned. In this position the barge is steered and helped ahead and slightly sideways if desired. I was soon in unison with the navigation down, anticipating orders while threading through the numerous channels left to us by the large number of sailing barges at anchor off Shadwell. Actually, old Bonsor (his nickname) hardly gave an order, I was already doing it. I knew, that he knew, that I knew. After this day my reception from him was much more cordial. This may sound trivial but my Father's one desire had been to make me efficient. I must add that today in 1935 in my particular firm very little indeed is the 'under oar' work that is carried on. With all due respect to the present youths of the river, who are really good material, there is no opportunity for similar training and also no demand, but to see a youth cuddling an oar, when handling, makes me feel like a drill sergeant watching an awkward squad.

The usual duties of an unlicensed apprentice in this employ were second hand to freemen in craft registered to carry above fifty tons, and boat boys rowing the river Foreman about his district. It would have been surprising to the Freemen had they known how well their characters and temperaments were discussed and realised by we apprentices. After receiving orders for a night's work with a Freeman, we would congratulate or commiserate with each other. I soon found that abstainers and temperate men were the best friends for a lad. They took an interest in one, were neater, cleaner and kinder. To spend a few hours of the night in a cabin with an effluvia exuding odour was unpleasant for a sensitive lad. The majority of men carried 'screws' (gimlets), and as cargoes were often wine, rum and gin, the drink was cheap. Tapping a cask could be done without showing any evidence from the outside. 'Do it clean' was the maxim, by gently tapping the hoops toward the tapering end, then boring two small holes. After the 'waxer' had been drawn, the holes were neatly spiled,[1] and the hoops hammered back over the holes and secured. At this period I was prejudiced against alcoholic drinks and although perhaps not offered, we apprentices had opportunities after the carousal to sample the drink, but the smell and fear of the stuff was sufficient for me. I must confess that I never refused a tin of 'pines' or similar goods.

Here is an acount of one night's work with a drunken man. I was sent to Victoria Dock to be second hand up with a barge laden with seventy tons of wheat to French's Mill at Bow Bridge. This meant going up the River Lea, or as it is termed, Bow Creek, which is tidal, the entrance being just above Victoria Dock. On my arrival at the Victoria Dock the barge was found among those first to come out and looking down into the cabin

[1] plugged

I saw the Freeman asleep. So without calling him I saw the barge into the lock, giving up the dock pass and shouting out the name to the 'booker out'. When ready to enter the river I attempted to call the man but although breathing, he was insensible. I could not draw back as the craft were hove out with a capstan rope. My age was between 15 and 16 and there was I underway with 70 tons of cargo. Without the least wish to boast, I was proud that we arrived at Bromley Lock after negotiating what was to me an immense responsibility. This would have lasted about four hours and although repeated calls were given, and attempts to awaken him, they were unsuccessful. At Bromley I again shouted down the cabin scuttle hatch; his eyes opened, and seeing that daylight had come he began to rate[1] me for coming so late. When, however, he got up and saw that we were moored just outside Bromley Lock, he asked who had brought the barge up. He then said, 'Don't stop any longer. Get home to breakfast, but don't tell any-one about this.' I promised, but could not keep it from Father, who, however, cross-examined me upon the night's navigation. I have refrained from mentioning the name of the Lighterman chiefly because some years later he was found drowned.

Our worst night out was to go as second hand to 'Big Nibby'. He was a mountain of flesh, fat everywhere, which made the eyes appear small. He was very nimble of foot considering the bulk, probably younger in years than our youthful estimation. Having acquired the knack of sleeping standing up, he would have several naps on the journey, holding the handle of the oar, blade flat, swaying and rocking to the swell. (I had read Pickwick at school, the fat boy 'asleep again'). When going to sleep in a cabin he would not, or perhaps could not, lie down. Sitting on the bench facing the fire he would sway sideways, backwards, then surge forward just missing the fire; at this point snorts and gurgles would be emitted, the performance being repeated the whole time of his being in the cabin. If a lad could find a 'better ole' he took the opportunity; some would rather face the cold than these porcine snorts.

There were other Freemen at this firm who were delightful to be underway with, never missing an opportunity to school the apprentice, but as one takes the rosy side of life as granted, the unpleasant episodes remain more vivid in one's memory.

Apart from river navigation, there were important duties expected of a Quay Lighterman, such as, full knowledge of Custom's regulations regarding bonded goods, free goods and transhipments. How to stow properly — and what was also important — how to sign for cargoes received, a covering clause being inserted on the Bill of Lading, or receipt, if the condition as received justified the signature offered. This knowledge was gradually acquired, and needless to say some men were real sea lawyers when arguing with the Mate of a ship regarding signatures. Sometimes one would be taken with the Freemen to watch the procedure; this would only happen if the man had a real interest in the apprentice.

---

[1] to scold angrily

3 THE LICENCED APPRENTICE 1896—1901

In Charge Under Oars

(I)
Nine Elms to the Tower

In August 1896 I obtained my licence; this is practically the same as a Freeman's except that of being unable to take an apprentice until the whole term of apprenticeship had been served. My duties were then principally that of being in charge of small craft (punts) loading cotchels[1] for various wharves, ships and docks. Being in sole charge one felt that one was really an important person.

Shortly after this event I was discharged. Our governor, Mr. Robert Gray, was incensed by having to pay a claim for broken marble slabs and he sacked all the apprentices. The facts were that an apprentice, well on in his time, had loaded some marble. The stowage should have been from each wing or long ways, fore and aft each side, leaning to its side and the middle space blocked off. In this instance the marble was stowed 'Burthen', that is athwartships, the bearing being taken from the bulkhead. When at London Dock inner lock the sluices were opened, causing strong eddies, the barge hit the pier head and marble slabs were transformed into marble rubbish.

At this time, a 'known to be well trained apprentice' could obtain employment easily, the reason being cheapness. If the employer cared to risk his property, the boy was allowed to do the same duties, except heavy loading and backing sacks of cargo, as a Freeman. The Trade Union today has restricted this. After this incident, I went back to the original employ where my first two weeks as an apprentice had been spent. Being now somewhat stouter and possessing the licence, I was startled by the men who remembered my first two weeks by remarking, 'This is young Harris. You knew what the governor said when he saw him at the office for his money, "Him a Lighterman? I felt as though I would pick him up in my arms and kiss him".' This was laughed off but never forgotten by my mates while in this employ.

The cargoes lightered by this firm were lead and glass, their wharf being at the upper part of Nine Elms, Farmiloes. Here was a good school for one to learn lightering as an above bridge man. As distinct from Quay Lightering, we were daily journeying on that part of the river between Battersea and the Pool. The above bridge man rather prided himself upon this special knowledge, and although good all round men worked at the 'quays', they were in a minority, so in some cases a voyage 'up through' was an adventure. Our men could tell immediately if a stranger to the usual 'up homers' was conversant with this navigation. Quay men were rather looked down upon by them as remarks like, 'two of gum and one of wax is all they know about', indicate.

---

[1]small quantities of cargo

I was congratulated for having the sense to come into a real lighterage job. The probability is that these 'above bridgers' would have found the other man's job equally as intricate.

The usual working of craft above bridge if double-handed was to send the junior aft to steer and, at the same time, by laying the oar well round the stern, help the head way. Every bridge with numerous arches was built on a bend in the river, such as Waterloo, Vauxhall, Battersea, Barnes and Kew. Here the tide would set away from the point. By slightly steering at an angle when shaping for a bridge hole, as the arch was called, the hand aft rowing against the man forward, a barge could be edged up against the tidal set as well as increasing the headway. Just before entering the hole the barge was straightened up and the bridge shot. After shooting Vauxhall on a strong spring tide, the barge would gather enough headway to shoot her into the wharf about a mile above without much effort, although a strong set of tide came off above Nine Elms Pier. If the wind was 'hard out of the wharf', and a stack of plate glass was the cargo, hard rowing and careful watching alone were the means of 'fetching' the wharf successfully.

When conversant at this work (I meant with), it was enjoyable. After shooting London Bridge the craft seemed to gather headway, and by just jogging on the oar when required, the barge would keep enough steering way until we arrived at the destination. I have gone aft at London Bridge and not been forward again until bringing up at the wharf. This was often done by regular traders, but the first time you decide to stay aft it requires some strength of mind not to run forward and give her a couple of 'Quick 'uns', especially when you saw the temporary Vauxhall wooden bridge with its narrow pigeon holes rushing towards you. Later this bridge was made more navigable by the removal of an arch, or rather the arch was widened by the removal of one of the piers.

The following detailed description of part of a day's work is one of the few memories that can be recorded, the reason being that for the first time I had a second hand a raw apprentice, this being his first day's work afloat. I have often had apprentices with me but this was this one's first initiation into barge work. The incidents are still fresh in my memory.

I had worked up with a single handed barge on the flood tide to our wharf, receiving orders there from the Foreman to take the 'Jubilee' to the Royal Albert Dock, the new boy as mate. Spring tides were running, high water in the afternoon. This was about five to six hours' journey so we had dinner and tea together before leaving — that is a cup of tea and extra jam tart after dinner. This had a good effect on our morale as although hungry and the coffee shops closed when we reached our destination, we have had our tea, although at 3p.m.

We started away from the wharf with the wind about south. My mate was very green. I was busily engaged in looking after him as the oar was unmanageable in his hands, I taking the pair with him hanging on to instruct him in the rhythm of swinging out and pulling steadily; he was really more trouble to me than the barge. I was real sorry for him, as he had rowed up with the skiff and blisters were now forming on both hands. We allowed her to blow over to leeward, I explained that usually we had to row across the river to the Pimlico shore to get in a favourable working position to shoot Vauxhall. As the river bends towards Vauxhall the wind leads from aft, and it was a fair wind to Waterloo on this day.

An elderly, be-whiskered 'hoveller' (pronounced 'huffler') is rowing his boat near us. Hoveller is the term applied to a waterman who acts as a bridge pilot to sailing barges up through the bridges. This one referred to was Tom Cunis, brother to Mr. R. Cunis the Master Lighterman. On reaching their destination they would assist in heaving up the mast and, on the return trip down along, would help raise it again at the mud-hole just above London Dock, Shadwell.

'Hello my old Banksider, and how are you, old man?' is the first greeting from him; he always prefixes with 'old man'.

'All right, Tom,' says I, 'how do you find things?'

'I don't know at all. Things ain't like they used to be, you know, old man. I remember … etc.' By this time he has come right alongside and having placed the sculls inboard is standing up in the board, or dish as he calls her, and leans both arms on our gunwale. He is aware that I am a patron of the Old Vic when not at work on Thursday nights.

'It was lovely old man, last night,' said Tom, 'A singer actually sung about me.'

'Go on, fancy that,' was something like my reply.

'Yes, old man, he sung about Lighterman Tom, and I shut my eyes and knew that he was singing it to me. Where are you going old man?'

'Down the Albert,' replied I in the vernacular.

'Well don't forget next Thursday it's the 'Bohemian Girl,' old man, have you seen it?'

'Never,' answered I. 'What is it all about?'

'You know the song, old man?' And here Tom sings the opening lines in a deep-throated voice of 'I dreamed that I dwelt'.

My mate who has been listening suddenly bursts into loud laughter. My suspicion is that he knows another version. The laughter draws old Tom's attention to the lad and signifying with his pipe he asks, 'New 'un?' I nod. 'Do I know him?', says Tom, meaning is he of the river. I shrug shoulders, being non-committal. 'It's a wonder where they find 'em. I don't know what's to become of me and you?' With a 'so long, old man', he settles down in his dish and paddles slowly away.

We are now on the north side opposite Nine Elms Pier. I spot a friend at the coal wharf adjacent. Giving a long whistle, an imitation of a starling, I draw his attention. Up shoots his arm and then a shout. I am not certain of the words but sense that it is 'Where are you going?' I wave down the river two from the elbow and one long one from the shoulder; he then knows that I am bound to somewhere in the lower reaches. This is a

Just below here a boat comes alongside our port side, a mop is shown over the stern to signify a buyer of old rope.

Friday and the gang always meet in the gallery at Gattis music hall, sometimes not getting there until 10pm, if working late. I raise my arms above my head waving them crosswise, scissor fashion; he now knows that this present job will prevent an appearance in the gallery tonight.

The tide is now beginning to run faster, and drawing the lad's attention to the nine arches of Vauxhall I point out the need to 'hold em up' to the north buttress of whichever arch you mean to work through. I take the oar aft for him and instruct him that when I say 'pull' to pull steadily and watch me. When I say 'give it to her' I mean pull as hard as you can. When you get the order 'the other way', reverse the oar at the stern post. There is now no time for talking, but our navigation is well in hand as we shoot No. 3 from the 'North'ard'. Just below is the temporary bridge, but this is easy now as the middle arch is fairly wide.

As we pass the Tate Gallery, drawing the lad's attention to the figure of Britannia, I ask him what is wrong with the figure? The answer is that Britannia is holding the Trident in the right hand, whereas on the penny it is shown the reverse way: which is correct is a matter for dispute. Probably the original die for the figure on the coin was in the right hand, this coming out on the reverse when stamped. This however is only a guess on my part. Just below here a boat comes alongside our port side, a mop is shown over the stern to signify a buyer of old rope. His behaviour is somewhat unusual, standing up and peeping furtively down the river, and we follow his glance and notice on the Lambeth shore the River Police rowing up over the tide. As his boat is on the blind side to anyone on the south shore, he can see by peeping over the gunwale and remain unseen from the south bank. When out of the angle of vision he rows away chanting 'Old rope!' Possibly his transactions today have been without reproach but he believes in safety first. Also I notice a sculler in a racing boat paddling up abreast of Doulton's Pottery. This is George Odell of Lambeth who is training for Doggett's.[1] I give the lad the benefit of my criticism of the rower: 'not quite the proper finish'. Hoping that he will turn out and row down alongside I give a well known whistle, but all we can hope to get is a turn of the head. This lad Odell won that year, so as a critic I had a lot to learn.

We are now at Lambeth Bridge, three arches only, my mate is getting his sea legs but not his river hands. I tell him not to look at them so often and he will forget them. The tide is by now full ebb and with a fresh breeze aft we are making good way: Lambeth Palace and later St. Thomas's Hospital on the south bank, the Houses of Parliament and Big Ben on the north. Pointing to St. Stephen's Tower I tell my mate that a small Union Jack flying there signifies Parliament is sitting as does a white light at night. I expect Guy Fawkes was mentioned but cannot remember now.

---

[1] Doggett's Coat and Badge Race rowed annually since 1715 for Watermen and Lightermen in the first year of their Freedom.

We are nearing Westminster Bridge and both of us are aft keeping her straight, as the tendency is for craft to come broadside to a wind. There is good way on her so pointing her to the centre of number four arch we take the middle. Attention of the lad was called to the cruel looking buttress here, edges like knives, shapes similar to a ship's ram; the lower the tide the more pronounced ram for awkward or unlucky people. A bundle of straw is hanging suspended in the centre of the arch. I explain this is a signal that repairs are being done at this spot to the bridge. When under the arch I gaze up into the staging; there is a painter pausing in his work looking down at our barge shooting through. Cupping both hands I yell so that the echoes ring (most bridges will produce an echo): 'What stinks worse than a painter?' A reply was expected, but not the reply, 'A dirty little barge boy!' He won. Here was I, in charge, with a new apprentice, patent to all observers, being actually considered by another workman a dirty little boy. I suffered from an inferiority complex for the next five minutes.

To regain my spirits I demonstrate to the lad how an oar should be handled. He is shown how to carry this from end to end of the craft, blade in water, speedily and safely, and, how to throw it 'for'ard' for steering. It is essential for this to be smartly and correctly accomplished. An oar can easily take charge of its owner, especially when the craft has good headway going through the water, such as when entering slack water from the tideway, similar in fact to a novice in a row boat 'catching a crab'. The 'feel' of how to handle an oar, in this case 28 feet long, comes by practice. A real smart operation is to shift the oar from the rowing tack or crutch to the opposite side in one movement around the bow. This is done by walking smartly 'forward' with the oar, blade tilted, causing the blade to be parallel with the handle, then placing the point of balance on the bitt head or fore post, weighing down on the handle, and with a semi-circular movement — hands, arms and feet working in unison — the oar is flung say from port side to starboard. This may appear a lot of words, but I can assure anyone who may be interested in river work that these essentials formed an important item of 'under oar' work.

Our barge has now begun to drift sideways during the lesson. We straighten her up just above Hungerford Bridge (Charing Cross). A sailing barge, mast on deck, sprit overhanging aft, mizzen set and drawing well, one man rowing, the skipper at the wheel, but no bridge sail or small lug set, quickly passes us. We notice 'Maldon' painted on the stern. There is not a hoveller in charge. This is rather unusual with an 'Essexman', their mode of procedure when without this pilot is to drop down with the tide, anchor dragging: this is termed 'gilling'.

The wind will shorten in the next reach. I have already decided to work No. 4 arch of Waterloo Bridge to be up to windward for the long stretch to Blackfriars. The set of tide at Waterloo on the ebb is distinctly consistent, hard set to north at all times of the ebb. We

The result was a glancing blow along our starboard side…

are now about halfway between Hungerford and Waterloo, mate aft, I for'ard edging her up to the south buttress of No. 4. The sailing barge, just below us, is in an excellent position to take this arch when suddenly he drops anchor 'all standing'. The effect caused by this action was that the 'Sailorman' suddenly swung round head upon tide, the mate paying away fathoms of cable hand over hand, the barge sheering about as though resentful of this treatment. We were in a direct line astern: the skipper at the helm was steadying the sheering endeavouring to avoid us, while we were shaping to avoid him. The result was a glancing blow along our starboard side, no damage to either, but we are transformed from a live ship into a drifting hulk. The blow had caused my mate to lose his oar, our barge to lose her headway and drift sideways, me to lose my temper but luckily for our governor, not losing my nut. We are almost at the bridge and though apparently in line for the arch I realise that with no headway, number 4 was a doubtful starter. This is all in the space of minutes and now is the time to decide, and when decided, act. Throwing the oar over to starboard I row hard to shape for number 3 arch, then reversing our only oar to the port side we row about a dozen hard ones to straighten up. My decision was if we have got to hit the bridge we will do so on the 'soft' side, as it is termed, this meaning the tide is setting from that side, as opposed to the 'hard' side with the tide setting on. With the wind now 'short' we are helped into number 3 arch just clear of touching. A spectator from the bridge

would have anticipated a 'side-winder'.[1]

There are now two things to do. Firstly, abuse the skipper of the Sailorman, who has by now hove up short, dropping gently down above the bridge. He is too far away to waste many words. He is told exactly in what part of the body I would have the pleasure of seeing him wearing that anchor. Secondly, to recover the lost oar. By manoeuvering head up on tide the oar was recovered, but our barge was on a lee[2] shore near the Embankment. It was hard slogging to Blackfriars, several tugs passed under our head giving us their flop flop wash which did not help matters, but we managed to row her out into the middle arch of Blackfriars.

In justice to 'Sailormen', as sailing barge people are called by lightermen, they are a fine type of river and coastal men. The incident just related is local, the skipper probably owner or part-owner decided to save the hoveller's fee, but when confronted with the numerous arches of Waterloo, was not sure of himself — safety first. The London River 'Sailorman' generally has, and should have better local knowledge than Essex and Rochester men, but as all round men, sailormen get there.

By now I am quite happy again after attempting to imitate the 'Essexman's' broad dialect. To spectators on a bridge the sight of two youngsters rowing a barge down river and bursting into laughter must have seemed strange. As we pass my birthplace I give the Bankside

[1]hitting buttress side on
[2]shore towards which the wind is blowing

The tide at this spot between Southwark and London Bridges, runs in my opinion, the fastest on the journey.

whistle. Uncle Alf waves. Several labourers at the old iron wharf wave also. St. Paul's is opposite. I ask the lad what is the height? Then, who was the architect? He learnt it at school but forgets. Later at the Monument when passing, the same questions. He was right about the height, but the architect also built Nelson's Column — name forgot!

All that I learnt about Sir Christopher Wren is related, so below Billingsgate St Dunstan's Spire is seen, and he is asked again. Quite right this time; again later at Limehouse Church. Limehouse St Anne's was built by a pupil of Sir Christopher Wren's. Greenwich College, I did not know then who was the architect or the founder, or perhaps had forgotten, but the lad knew — Sir Christopher Wren, one of his finest works. I believe if Tower Bridge had been mentioned, Wren would have been responsible!

At Southwark Bridge his attention is called to the three lamps that in those days marked the centre of the middle arch. By passing to the 'south'ard' of these, just on our port quarter, we shall work into Cannon Street Arch without trouble. The tide at this spot between Southwark and London Bridges, runs, in my opinion, the fastest on the journey. There are several races of tide such as off Rosherville, Gravesend, but this rather narrow straight shoot of tide is always like a mill race. At this time of ebb tide there is a tidal set to the south at the middle of London Bridge but at or from half ebb to low water the direction changes from a straight shoot through to one hard to the north buttress. Memory does not serve for the rest of this journey as I want to record actual facts. The next part of the journey from London Bridge to Royal Albert Docks will be a description of those times as seen from a barge.

The river below London Bridge to Cherry Garden is called the Upper Pool. The reach below to Limehouse is the Lower Pool. At this period the majority of trade from Continental and Coastal steamers was lightered from vessels lying at the Tiers.[1]

Fresh Wharf was a hive of industry, chiefly cargoes from the Mediterranean and the Near East — Turkey, Greece and Alexandria. The Dutch trade was at Custom House and Brewers Quay. Treport steamers at Hay's Wharf, load afloat; Ghent steamers to and from Mark Browns Wharf. A Gravesend trader, the 'Witch', a steam hoy traded between St Olave's Wharf and Gravesend. There was one tier on the south side, above Tower Bridge; Battle Bridge chiefly used by steamers from Dunkirk. On the north side the tiers above Tower Bridge were upper and lower Brewers Quay. Mooring chains called Yarmouth Chains just above; this was for small craft, schooners etc. Below Tower Bridge to Cherry Garden on the south side, tiers were German Hamburg, Norwoods, Mill Stairs, Upper East Lane, Lower East Lane and Fountain. Except the first mentioned, the principal user was the General Steam Navigation Company with Antwerp, Charente and other continental trade. On the north side, Irongate Buoy (Hull, Yarmouth, Ostend), Dublin Buoy (Jersey);

[1] bouyed ship moorings

Every quay lighterage firm had its boat

Hermitage upper, Lower Hermitage and Union Tier, (Antwerp, Dantzig, Hamburg and Dunkirk trade). Today this trade is done from the docks and wharves with modern jetties and facilities for motor lorry traffic. There is still considerable water-borne business from these ships, but land traffic has today competed with us in taking goods direct to the ship's side. Every ship at a Tier had her attendant craft off-loading, or shipping exports. Each landing stairs had regular watermen plying for hire chiefly to and from these ships. Apart from barges, there were rowing boats everywhere in this part of the Pool. I can only remember the following services who had steam launches: Thames Conservancy, Police ('Chowkidar' and 'Watch'), and a small launch called 'Tynesider' belonging to a dry dock company. Every quay lighterage firm had its boat, and the more important ones had two boat boys. Some, perhaps for economy, had the foreman rowing himself.

Everyone knew everybody else. A boat could be recognised long distances away. Some foremen never sat, others huddled. Some would never take an oar, others often 'spelled'[1] the lad or lads when rowing over the tide. The colours of the firms or companies painted on the blades could be recognised and word was soon flashed that 'he' was about. Each firm had its own distinctive whistle. Two foremen in particular were good performers emitting something like a lark's song would be in quick motion.

The River Police were in row boats, the blades painted white. You could see them in the dark anywhere. These were later painted drab or khaki. In the absence of watermen during the night, the Police would take lightermen off their craft, but this was rather expensive. I had a ride ashore on one occasion with them at the expense of 1/- — my next day's dinner money! The impression being the same of all waterside people that lightermen worked day and night and were always 'well breeched'. The Customs had their rowing boats, some two rowers, others three. The Surveyor had a four oared cutter, a real smart turn out. The crew were always piling their oars blades forward. The Captain Superintendent of the G.S.N.C. had his boat with two watermen (Captain Ellis). His picture is now hung in their offices at Tower Hill. His Labour Master had one waterman. The coal foremen also had a boat with one waterman. The whole Pool was well served with row boats. Old ropies, beer boats, drudger boats for recovering coal knocked overboard (or borrowing it before that advent), under-watermens' boats for recovering anchors and jetsam.

As we pass under Tower Bridge we look for a passing horse omnibus, several of these having 'box' seats each side of the driver. Invariably the passenger next to the driver was a member of the fair sex. We would then whistle 'Mary is young and fair, she rides upon my bus in dear old London.' This was always received as a compliment, the driver saluting by 'dipping the whip'.

---

[1] give someone a break

In Charge Under Oars

II
The Tower to the Royal Albert Dock

Looking back on those days the remaining impression is that of light hearted days. We found fun all the time, hours were long, work was strenuous, but I cannot remember any occasion of dissatisfaction with my sphere in life. Summertime always compensated for winter.

South Devon Wharf just below St. Katherine's Dock was the home of trading hoys and sailing craft loading for Margate, Ramsgate and Sandwich. This place is mentioned in W. W. Jacobs' yarns. He used to take trips from here in these craft, although called by him 'The Wharf'. The nightwatchman here was an old bargee. As we near the Wapping entrance of London Dock care is taken to hold our barge up to the point, a hard set to the south'ard takes place here. Just above the point is the site of 'Execution dock'. St John's Wharf was built on the spot. I have no authority for stating this except verbal statements from old lightermen when I was a boy. Here, according to their accounts, pirates were executed, the bodies left for three tides to cover (as pirates were tough to kill). A covering of pitch and tar was put over the bodies, these being transported by water to Blackwall Point to be suspended from a gibbet as a warning to mariners against piracy. On the south side are moorings 'Cherry Garden Chains' for several tiers of schooners and ketches. Here the china clay from Cornish ports was discharged into lighters. Then on the same side Church Hole tiers, upper and lower. These were used by large ships from all parts. Copper ore, magnesite ore, guano and esparto grass being the usual cargoes. The opposite side, from Tunnel Pier to the 'Prospect of Whitby' (an old time pub with overhanging balcony) is known as the 'Mud Hole' used as an anchorage by sailing barges. This unpleasant incident was witnessed by me off there.

While rowing past Tunnel Pier with a barge, the body of a drowned person came to the surface with impetus, the arms above the head slightly bent gave the appearance of its rising higher out of the water than could have been possible, a bow to the river that had taken him, resignation being registered by the movements as it slowly settled into the floating position. Without being too gruesome 'deaduns' were common sights on the riverside. I have been the means of saving life while at work but only getting wet once. Although not as spectacular, a rescue from a dry position, if possible, is the sanest course for rescuer and rescued. At the end of the Lower Pool the river bends to the right, Cuckold's Point (Cockles). As at all points the tide sets hard away to the bight, with a westerly breeze, making the Millwall side a lee shore. Careful nursing here is required to fetch through to where the river again bends left. In the whole of this work the wind was an

With all sails drawing on a beam wind

important factor. Before one started up or down he would form a mental plan, perhaps automatically, of the course to be taken, where to let her fall away to get a wind advantage or where to nurse her up to be right up to windward for the next reach. This part of Rotherhithe with 'Cockles' Point as the apex is or was called 'Down Town'. It was right off the map from the highway, the Surrey Docks between. The waterside inhabitants were called 'Down Towners', families inter-marrying for generations. I have been told of people there who only on rare occasions ever left this district for any purpose. Just below the point was the Smallpox Pier where patients were taken by steamer to the floating hospital at Dartford, half way down Long Reach. There were three of these piers, Fulham, Rotherhithe and Blackwall. On the left bank are the Limehouse entrances to the South and West India Docks. These entrances were closed before 1894. I can remember one being open before my apprenticeship. These docks are at right angles to the river, the Blackwall entrances opening out into Blackwall Reach. This reach is the opposite bearing to Limehouse, running north by east, Limehouse bearing south, south west. The South West India Dock was originally a canal formed to make a quicker passage avoiding the detour round the 'Isle of Dogs' (City Canal). The vessels lying in these docks are almost all sailing ships, a veritable forest of masts and spars showing right through to Blackwall. Men are seen high aloft working in the rigging. This is a specialised occupation, they are riggers. These men know all the intricate working of the gear of a full rigged ship. The chief trade of sailing vessels from here and the East India Dock was to Australia, New Zealand and San Francisco calling at Chilean ports. Just below the West Dock is Chalkstones Buoys. These moorings were used by large coasting sailing barges.

We pass Millwall Dock on our left and the Greenland entrance of the Commercial Dock on the right. The river bends left here until we open Blackwall Reach. The tide sets to the 'south'ard' from Millwall Dock to Cubitt Town Point, we working our barge all the time to the north bank. At Cubitt Town we shall allow her to fall over to East Greenwich, thus getting the full run of tide and also to save hard rowing at Blackwall Point. Greenwich College and the Observatory on the hill are on the right bank with the Almshouses just below. Fishing smacks are moored on the foreshore facing the Almshouses, several at this time working from Greenwich. If any sailing barges were underway, now would be the time to see them as live creatures. With all sails drawing on a beam wind, contrasting with the 'gilling' so much detested by the lightermen then and by the tug master in 1935. We should, according to the season, have now met pleasure boats either out or homeward bound. In a crowded reach with 'sailormen' tacking and lighters 'driving', meaning drifting broadside, occasioned by adverse wind when it was impossible to hold a lighter head on, there would be scanty room for a large paddle steamer to work through. We always, if apparently in the way under these circumstances, 'squared her up' pulling the lighter stern on wind, thus presenting the lighter end on as opposed to broadside. The Captain would often come to the end of his bridge and acknowledge the effort with a salute of the hand. Captain Mills of the 'London Belle' was a fine type; to see him lift his hand to the right temple and hear 'thanks old man' in his deep voice, with a holiday cargo of passengers as spectators, was real thanks.

On the Cubitt Town shore right on the point was 'Mouth Organ Wharf' (Grosvenor Wharf). The machinery used in manufacturing block fuel caused weird noises, proving also a good guide in foggy weather.

I must wander from this journey at the mention of fog. The river then becomes a black area, if one was suddenly caught; it depended upon circumstances such as loaded or light craft, time of tide, destination, also 'push and go' whether you attempted to proceed with the barge or found the first safe mooring. Where one would never start in a dense fog, but if caught in one, might carry on and be lucky to finish the job, the ears became eyes, and all senses alert to get a bearing, yelling out to anchored craft 'Where are you?' You may get a bearing from this, but sometimes it was 'you ought to be locked up being underway in this weather.' When at this present job, we did not get underway with loaded craft in foggy weather except perhaps for small journeys in the Pool, but never did we refrain from getting under way in the daytime fog with empty craft. By tying

several knots in the end of the anchor chain we would 'gill' down the river, the dragging chain keeping us head upon tide, checking the barge, the tide running past giving us headway. With the oar for'ard for steering and if double handed one aft, all ears for the traffic noise at the first bridge, the first glimpse of anything solid or a light was taken to advantage, quick steering, or perhaps the hand aft would yell 'stand hard' as we slide through perhaps a glancing blow as she cleared.

I remember a job in the winter of 1903 because it was the only time my pay sheet was questioned. I expected medals. My orders were 'Edwin' loaded with iron, Free Trade Wharf to Fulham Steel Works. Leaving Free Trade at low water about 3 p.m. weather bad, visibility about middle to shore or tiers, the rope was frozen similar to stiff wire, the head sheets[1] covered with frozen snow. I obtained a piece of grating to stand upon and tied sacking around the oars as the rowing parts were icy. Darkness came on at about Tower Bridge, the fog also descended, a real thick 'un. The 'Edwin' had no anchor but there was a long chain headfast. This was run overboard to check her head upon tide. I decided to 'turn it up' but was unable to 'fetch' the buoy at Paul's Wharf. The next object was the piles around Blackfriars Bridge; repairs to the bridge were taking place. Getting clear of these I found the boats moored below the training ship at the Temple but fortunately no damage was done to them. Still gilling up all along the Embankment where an occasional halo of light gave me

[1]fore-deck of lighter

30

the sense of direction, I successfully negotiated the two Vauxhall Bridges. The next light after this was Nine Elms Pier. Rowing for the old wharf I tied her up there. Seeing a glimpse of a barge light I re-started; Chelsea Reach and Fulham was to me a black wall. Finding the wharf at last with the moorings run overboard in the mud, to be fished up and overhauled to find the end, I finished at 8.40 p.m.

Then horse tram to Southwark, home about 10 p.m. A short night was charged by me viz: 4/- — that is from 8-12 p.m. This was stopped as in the foreman's opinion I had ample time to be done by 8 p.m. This was ultimately paid!

Fog is the worst enemy of the river work. Signs of fog can be observed but indications of its clearing other than a breeze are very few. I have said good night to our foreman at 12.30 p.m., having orders to take 'one' to Battersea, two hours before high water and a dense fog; he going home expecting the job to be a 'baulk'![1] A sudden lift of the fog and one hour and a half of real slogging gave him a pleasant surprise in the morning. We now return to Blackwall Reach. The buoys on the left side are 'Folly House buoys'. A large fore and aft rigged ship is discharging turpentine and resin into lighters. Below here is Yarrow's Yard, several torpedo boats being under construction there. Below this again is Watkins' Hulk, the mooring for the tugs of that firm who in those days used Blackwall as their headquarters. At Blackwall Point the river bends right into Bugsby's Reach. Over in the bight is the East India Dock, again a

forest of masts and spars. Several tugs with craft in tow would have passed us, usual greetings and signs exchanged with the men in charge, or in our language 'chipping'. Every young lighterman seemed in those times to be happy, probably the physical fitness acquired by hard exercise in the fresh air caused this exuberance of spirits. Every incident was a subject of mirth. I have tried to remember really angry moments in those days, but they are so few to be beyond·recall. The sailorman at Waterloo is one.

We are now passing Bow Creek with the Trinity Wharf at one side, the Thames Ironworks opposite. A 'lightship' undergoing repairs would be lying at the Trinity, her name in large white letters painted on her side. At the Ironworks a huge battleship on the stocks towering above any other object (HMS Albion). A deafening clattering of rivets being hammered flat would drown other noises. Then Victoria Dock with Cory's dummy the upper side of the entrance. Just a little lower down on the Charlton side were the coal derricks, one and two. Coals were discharged then from ships moored here. If a soft coal was being unloaded, clouds of coal dust would be observed rising. A passing tug running back light to Victoria Dock would have a gang of 'Coalies' on her deck returning ashore, having been relieved. They would be covered in dust, the lips showing red as cherries, the dust having been washed off by the application of the tea bottle, the whites of the eyes also a contrast to the all black appearance. If near enough to us we would whistle 'Whist, here comes the

[1] uncompleted job

bogeyman', but all coalies then appeared aged and repartee was not their strong point. Below the derricks the training ship 'Warspite'lay — an old wooden wall. When passing her in the evening and with several lads on her deck they would semaphore to us with their arms, this causing loud laughter among them. This was probably something uncomplimentary to a lighterman. Having had no training in semaphore we had to guess the compliments. By whistling 'A life on the ocean wave', then going through the performance of washing the hands and dropping them smartly palms down, we would try to convey that as sailors they were 'washouts'.

We are now in Woolwich Reach, the dockyard is on our right, the usual wharves on the north bank, iron, chemicals, pickled wood, cable, sugar, stone, flour, old iron, with Foster's beer just above the Ferry. Below the Ferry, the piers of Woolwich Arsenal with the big crane showing boldly and overtopping the wharf, came into view on the south side. The river bends left into Gallions Reach, just on the point is a favourite anchorage for sailing barges. We must go as near to them as safety allows as our entrance to R. A. Dock is 'under' the point. This is always a hard slog to get in, with a westerly wind dead out it was real hard work to fetch, but by careful 'nursing' and edging, also by watching all points of gaining ground to avoid the hard set-off you could make fast at the entrance thankful that you were not in mid stream as probably you would be watching someone rowing his heart strings out owing to careless 'shaping' for the dock. If in time for the coffee shop, one hoped that his 'two of dripping' would have plenty of gravy on its surface. If not, a glass of sour ginger beer from a tub, a biscuit, cheese and piccalilli or onions.

Having been employed at this firm for five years the work on the river to me was 'second nature'. One felt a delight in mastering a job that on first thoughts seemed hardly possible. And behind all this was that sense of duty and service to one's employers so thoroughly ingrained by Father. At this period I had several offers of employment, which if I could re-live would be accepted if only for the varied experiences, but that sense of duty kept me loyal to this firm.

4 FREEMAN OF THE WATERMEN AND LIGHTERMEN'S COMPANY 1901

In August 1901 I obtained my Freedom. Attending the Court of Watermen at Watermen's Hall and taking the oath with three other young lightermen holding a corner of the Bible, the Freedom was presented, the examination was confined to the name of my employers; this was sufficient. A member of the Court asked was I Charlie Harris's son; congratulations and my papers.

Having had one week's work as a fully licensed man, the foreman broke it gently that as things were slack and I was a very young Freeman, "You must stand off for a bit, taking your share of the work with the other men". This was quite fair because I was taking the same money as them but I resented being casual and although very boyish looking for twenty-one I had no fear of any job in river work. A Mr. Taylor of E. W. Taylor & Co. had always chatted to me when meeting him about the river area, hearing that I was 'off' he offered me a job guaranteeing regular employment. So within two days I commenced employment there. My former employer was annoyed when I told him on the pay night and I believe thought me ungrateful but realising today what we apprentices did for very low money perhaps he was ungrateful. Anyhow, I told him that I had left because regular work was promised. This promise was fulfilled, working for Messrs. Taylor the whole eight years following, without any lost time. This caused bad feeling among the hands at first, but after this had blown away I had eight happy years with real good practical lightermen. Our money was £2 per week, night work extra. This firm was a mixture of quay work and rough goods trade, the barges having to be taken to parts and wharves that although I knew the sites and positions on the river of these, the actual working to these places was entirely new to me. Therefore, after my apprenticeship was served I was still learning the river. The peculiar feature of riverwork was that a man may have only done one class of work all his life and watermen being very conservative they would if looking for fresh employment take a job in that class, never dreaming of changing.

My chief recreations just before and about this age were the Old Vic Thursday night, Gattis Music Hall Friday night, and about 1902 or 1903, Sunday League Concerts at the Allhambra or Queens Hall. If not at work these would be eagerly looked forward to. Gattis, Westminster Bridge Road, George Chirwin the white-eyed Kaffir, after being 'Blind Boyed'[1] as usual, sang instead:

---

[1] 'Blind Boy' a popular song George Chirwin was always requested to sing.

Sing up for Gattis,
Cheer up for Gattis,
Why make life a load,
Sing up for Gattis,
You know where that is,
Down in Westminster Bridge Road!

This was typical of him. His extempore work was very clever and topical. We would meet in the left hand corner of the gallery facing the stage, being well known to the artistes. If a lady turn winked at the boys she was sure of a good chorus from us. If we were resented by the rest of the audience, we won. Every turn was booked for three weeks, three songs and encores; it was possible to learn a song if one could get there three Fridays. I saw Sir Harry Lauder on his very first appearance as an extra. He went the same week to the Tivoli, but Gattis was his first music hall proper appearance in London.

The entrance fee was sixpence, the ticket was punched by the attendant; this taken to the bar would be worth twopence. I often had two Banbury cakes. The relief of Mafeking, on the 18th May 1900, was announced from the stage on one of these Fridays during the Boer War. Kate Carney the Coster singer emptied the house by announcing the news. Public houses closed then at 12.30 a.m. Several were compelled to close earlier on that occasion owing to their stocks having run out.

I commenced to drink wine when about 21 honestly thinking that I was a tee-totaller still. It is really more potent than most alcoholic drinks, and at this time two two's of port (twopence per glass) would make one loyal and patriotic to an excitable degree.

London went crazy that night, I returning home very early on the Saturday morning after attempting to walk the parapet that used to run outside the iron railings at Southwark Bridge.

My friends were many, any number up to ten meeting on evenings when not at work. We young lightermen were rather clannish and somewhat despised the 'landsman' or 'linen draper'. The chief topic was the river or work on the river. This had a language of its own so I presume that our shore friends were often fed up by attempting to listen to an account of an incident in the days' work given in the vernacular. You either 'fetched' or 'went by'; 'saved tide' or 'lost tide'; 'went clear' or 'athwart hawse'. Arches were called 'bridge holes' or 'working locks'. A Brentford man if bound to Brentford would be going 'right out'. A Battersea man would be bound 'up home'. A coal lighterman would be going 'down the Derrick'. Flood tide work was 'bound up along', ebb the reverse. The point was the 'pint'. The Quay man would be bound to 'K Dock', or 'the German', the 'Batty', down the Vic and dock her or perhaps 'Jack's hole'. The creek always called 'crick'. Back-slang was often used, cabin becoming nibac and so on.

A large number of lightermen went by nicknames, all very apt, either featuring physical or psychological defects or assets, such as Tubby, Podge, Narrow, Rasher, Dabtoe, Winkle-eye, Hoppy, Humpy and

Wiggy. Little Biggie was a tiny man of that name. Man Green was the smallest ever. Titty Mummy was about six foot two and big in proportion. Happy Wright, Bosco Deacon, Whisper Rivers, Moaner, Doctor Brooks, Mad Brady, Bonsor Corps, Knocker, Knacker, Knicker, Sancho, Pongo, Walloper, Curly, Gingers, Coppers and Snowies. Robinsons were Cockies, Blythes were Nellies, Hopkins and Perkins, Pollys. Mashers, Starchies, Stiffies and Rum and Rags. Fireworks, Redhot, Burn'em, Never Sweat, Dozey, Slowman, Squibs, Gentle Annie, Soft Roe and Pretty. Wooden Weight's name was earned in this manner. He used to supply coals by barge to sailing ships for fuel, the coal being weighed by scales in the barge's hold. The barge sank on one occasion, one of the weights being found floating next morning.

'A full roadun' was a week's work including Sunday and nights. A 'thgin' (tidgeon) was an easy night; Carman's night or Early Turn Out was to be ordered for 2/- at 5 a.m. between the radius of Victoria dock and Nine Elms. Tarpaulins were cloths, extra rope a warp, oars paddles and a pump was the organ. Tugs were 'toshers', the space aft of the cabin bench was 'Yarmouth Roads'. Anchor the 'Killick'. If a lighterman had a 'waxer' (cheap drink) for a friend, he would be told that 'there was one behind the pump.' The dock official whose duties were to enforce charges on craft when incurred was and is still the 'Bogie Man'. A 'brief' is still the return half of a railway ticket eagerly sought for at the lower docks if the holder was going back with craft; 'Got any briefs?' is often the first question when meeting a friend. 'Stand hard' is a caution to look out and stand firm, or crouch, holding on tight if the blow is going to be heavy. The 'ditch' is the river, 'fell in the ditch' is falling overboard. 'Gutsers', 'sidewinders', 'chimers', 'stern butt' (always a more vulgar term is used) and 'glancing blow' were terms describing blows to craft either by collision with other craft, or themselves colliding with a fixed object.

When reporting damage a man would often say 'just a glancing blow' especially if he was responsible. These were viewed suspiciously by the foremen. I worked under a man to whom this term was a 'red rag'. Lightermen were ever optimistic!

When I was about twenty-three, without warning I fell in love with the most winsome girl I had ever met. We knew each other as youngsters going to the same school but were never friendly then. We married in June 1906. I find it hard to express in writing my appreciation of her, cheerful, sympathetic, loving, a real mate and the best pal in life. A happy marriage, as ours has proved, is one of life's chief blessings.

In 1903 and 1904 I went Swan Upping, rowing stroke oar in the 'King's' boat. This is a journey by boat from Southwark Bridge to Marsh Lock, Henley to mark and pinion the young cygnets of that year. A company of six boats with three Swanmasters in charge, King's Vintners' Co. and Dyers' Co. The King and those companies are the owners of all swans in the area mentioned. Thirteen watermen manned the skiffs, the King's Swanmaster's boat having three, rowing randan.[1] The first day was Southwark to Hampton, then Hampton to Staines, Staines to Maidenhead, Maidenhead to Henley. Friday, Henley to Staines, finishing at Hampton Court Saturday. The pay was 10/- per day. This was looked upon as a holiday. The cygnets were piniored and marked by the Masters. King's Mark is a double diamond on the flat of the bill. Vintners' a nick in each corner of the bill. Dyers' a nick on one side only. When piniored, a swan is unable to fly properly; the nearest approach is a rapid skim over the water. This operation was done by the Swanmaster, one of us holding a wing, pulling the 'flight' out to right angles to the body. The Master would feel with his finger nail for the end joint or tip of the wing and with a sharp penknife sever the end. The wound was then dressed with Stockholm Tar and down plucked from its breast and wound around the cut.

The procedure of the day was all start together and row in a line, the smartest pair without the Master being 'top boat'. After the second day the top boat took its place without challenge. My mate was Ralph Hasler, we both being 'colts' or first timers were top boat for these two years, perhaps not the smartest pair but the most keen couple for that position. When a pair of swans with a brood were sighted, orders would be given as to the exact spot to pick them up, always choosing if possible a suitable landing. The boats would come along on the opposite side of the selected place, heading the

birds off and gradually edging them over. The top boat would shoot right ashore, the others all having their bows inside the quarters of each other, the bottom boat backing water, forming a crescent slowly lessening by pulling the boats up alongside of each other. The top boat men would have been ashore by now and with the hands picking up the swans and brood, by tying the feet over the tail and placing them in the bank for the Master to examine the marks on the parent birds caused some splashing and excitement. The cygnets were given the same marks as the parents. If the parents were not the sole property of one company, the young were shared. If an odd number brood, the odd cygnet was declared to belong to the male bird. A hand would sing out 'King's cob', 'Dyers' pen', 'Vintners' cob' or 'King's pen'; the cob is the male and pen the lady. I should mention that the cry given to the boats when closing for picking up was 'all up!'; this was a password among swan-uppers. I have often met an old hand when at work and even today 'all up' is the greeting.

The uniform worn was scarlet jacket with brass buttons, red jersey, white ducks (King's). Blue jacket with badge, blue and white striped jersey and white ducks (Vintners'). Blue jacket with badge, blue jersey (Dyers'). When arriving at Windsor the other companies formed lines and piled oars, the King's two boats rowing between and taking the salute. At Windsor we had 'Rootybranch'. The Vintners' Company would

---

[1] stroke and bow rowing one oar each and the one between them a pair

36

In 1903 and 1904 I went Swan Upping

be three on a launch, all the swan-uppers invited to the cabin, the master Mr. Abnett poured a glass of wine for each one who had to toast, "Here's to the Vintners' Company, root and branch!" Some gave it as above, but 'Rootybranch' was the usual.

Our evenings were spent in singsongs at the local and as most of us were in a holiday mood the nights were merry. The custom of 'loping' the 'colt' and bumping him on an old city stone at Staines was always carried out the two years that I went 'swan-upping'. The 'loping' was a baptism in the river, the old hands watching for an opportunity to take the 'colt' or newcomer unawares to push him overboard. It was fatal to be caught standing. A good trick was to place the blade of an oar between the colt's shoulder blades; one firm push and into the ditch he would go, the rest of the company giving loud cheers. The most keen of the old hands to do the loping were those that had been loped the previous year. I had a full share of both and sometimes jumped in for the fun of the diversion, especially after 'rootybranch'. Swan-uppers' wives and friends would be at Waterloo station to welcome them home on Saturday evening, the spoils of the chase being distributed among them, flight feathers from the tip of wings were lustily pulled out from the swans, these were worn in the hat, the effect being rather rakish. The swan can give a heavy blow with its wings especially with the wing that had ben pinioned when young. A knob of hard bone forms where the severance had taken place, but although the attitude of these birds when with their cygnets appears threatening, there is no danger to a determined person who picks them up and by tying the feet over the tail imprisons the wings, rendering the swan impotent. I have read of fierce swans, but other than a thump on the toe, the chief excitement was the splashing occasioned, especially at Windsor when it was common to pick up about thirty birds in one catch, these being all young cobs. The sexes are determined by the size of the protuberance in front of the head, the male showing a large bump or swelling. Swan-upping still takes place but the boats are towed by launch practically the whole journey. The contrast of the Upper Thames to the Lower was appreciated by the 'swan-uppers' in those days; the varied scenery being a good topic over a glass for the winter evenings.

The watermen and lightermen of my youth were proud of their river knowledge. Credit was always given to a skilful man, to be judged by your peers and the verdict 'he's a good lighterman' was gratifying to one who had made his work a pride. If one earned this epithet it was known among the fraternity with the result that employment could in a sense be chosen. The youths whose parents and perhaps much farther back were on the river were usually more apt to become handy men. I believe that the critical eye of these parents, uncles, cousins, neighbours etc. was a big incentive to these lads to whole-heartedly work and learn everything possible required to make them 'shape as a lighterman'. As a class they were loyal to each other, jealous of the 'privilege' (Freedom of the River), clannish as the clans, mildly tolerant of landsmen, benevolent to anyone in trouble. By holding a benefit concert for a widow or man in distress, fairly large sums in those days were collected. I could tell a lighterman anywhere, Sunday or day clothes apparel. The important articles of dress were good boots and good overcoats. Boots were pegged or sewn, a glance at a man's boots would tell who was the builder. Every riverside district had its shoemaker, this caused heated arguments as to the merits of each. The essential quality of an overcoat was to be warm and almost waterproof, a good test was to have about 8 hour's rain on a coat then to stand it up alone. I have seen this done, just a little dampness underneath the arms otherwise dry underneath. I believe the cloth used was either box cloth or Melton. This garment was also our blanket when turned in to rest in the cabin; this accounts for the number of men seen with coats on the arm at all seasons of the year. The training in those times gave the lighterman an important sense of command; he was in charge, no one to appeal to, the river often presenting problems which called for a decision with only one answer. The average sea-going man does not or did not understand the mentality of the lighterman and I am sure that it is this sense of 'I'm in charge' that makes lightermen appear to be hard headed and cocksure.

The Brentford man was of a different type, rather rural in outlook and appearance. Whiskers were worn on the chin only, the usual cloth used for clothing was a drab tweed, the waistcoat being made as part of the trousers. 'Coat and waistcoat all in one' was a term used to signify a Brentonian, although trousers and waistcoat in one were the facts. The 'Waremen' were those people in charge of craft that brought cargoes from the Upper River Lea in Hertfordshire. They were allowed to trade from the Lea to London without being licensed men or having a licensed man in charge. This was done under an old charter granted to them for services in London during the plague times when carriers were chary of entering the city. At this moment there are no Ware craft left, this work being carried out by a large company who still employ the relics of the community as bargemen. The cabins of the old craft were spotless, a mat was always on top to be used before entering.

I once had a narrow sqeak at Vauxhall Bridge owing to the action of a 'Wareman'. With enough way on his handy long barge of 60 tons to shoot the eye of a needle, he suddenly dropped anchor almost in the bridge hole on a hot spring flood tide. Three being the crew. I was single handed following him with fifty tons of girders, the lengths overhanging the cabin top. How she came away into the next arch is hard to realise now, but after striking him in passing I knew that if my course was not immediately altered, my barge would have broken in half upon striking the bridge. The lesser evil was decided upon, this becoming a blessing as my barge grazed through on the soft side with just a few splinters torn from the gunwale as she roared through. So it can be

'*The Lighterman, he was in charge, no one to appeal to…*'

quite understood that lightermen had but little respect for these men as tidal navigators. This incident, also the one on the ebb tide at Waterloo, are or were not exceptional happenings. A man working regularly in 'up thro' work would certainly meet at a tricky spot occasional situations where a rapid and correct decision acted upon would save heavy damage, or perhaps with loaded craft on strong tides, total loss.

In May 1909 I was approached by Mr. Scanlan who was then Tilbury Dock Foreman for H. Grey Jn. with a view to having an interview with his people with the object of getting employment on the staff of that firm. I later found out that Mr. Woodward (a partner) had asked him to nominate suitable candidates. The interview was arranged, I being appointed as Assistant Foreman London Dock. This appointment meant 'getting out of the rut' of a journeyman's life but it also meant long hours and very exacting governors. Here was I to learn 'dockology' and 'mancraft', the responsibility expected seemed unfair then. Our governors had a saying if one was excusing anything that had not gone as expected, ''we are all judged by results''. I tried, and believe, gave satisfaction, but although happy at work I was not happy in my work and often longed for the old days. I appreciate now that the training then was excellent, Mr. Thomas Woodward and Mr. George Woodward being without possible exception, the keenest businessmen ever connected with the lighterage trade.

I was later put in full charge of London Dock Dept., then transferred to Tilbury Dock where in 1935 I am extremely fond of my work and enjoy every day. The troubles that occur in business are no more or less than one's neighbours' misfortunes, so by counting our blessings, one looks forward to the next day. When perhaps in the mood I shall record in writing something about my life as a foreman or if not, I will conclude by accepting the truth of Father's words that, it is better to be a 'teller' than a 'told'.